Endpapers: a European world map, printed in 1570.
The Americas and Africa are shown; to the south is
the *Terra Australis nondum Cognita* the unknown land
to the south.

Library of Congress Cataloging-in-Publication Data

Kramer, Ann.
  Exploration and empire.

  (Historical atlases)
  Summary: Describes historical and social events in
various world nations during the period of exploration
and exploitation from 1450 to 1760.
  1. History, Modern—Juvenile literature. [1. History,
Modern] I. Title. II. Series.
D208.K73 1990 909.08 89-24892
ISBN 0-531-19074-9

Published in 1990 by Warwick Press,
387 Park Avenue South, New York, New York 10016.
First published in 1989 by Kingfisher Books Ltd.
Copyright © Grisewood & Dempsey Ltd. 1989.

Library of Congress Catalog Card No. 89-24892
ISBN 0-531-19074-9

Editor: Nicola Barber
Series editor: Ann Kramer
Series designer: Robert Wheeler
Cover design: Nigel Osborne
Maps: Eugene Fleury and Malcolm Porter
Illustrations: Kevin Maddison and Stephen Conlin
Picture research: Elaine Willis
Printed in Spain

HISTORICAL ATLAS

EXPLORATION & EMPIRE

Empire-builders, European Expansion & the Development of Science

Ann Kramer and Simon Adams

WARWICK PRESS

Contents

Introduction

This book covers the history of the world from the Renaissance to the eve of the Industrial Revolution. It examines the end of the great Aztec and Inca Empires, the great age of exploration, the growth of world-wide trade, European expansion, early settlement of the Americas, and the rise of the brilliant empires in China and Japan.

But history is not just about dates and events. It is also about people and how they lived in the past. Using clear maps and colorful illustrations, *Exploration and Empire* takes a close look at the daily lives of people during this period and describes how events changed their lives and took them into the beginnings of a modern world.

Exploration and Empire is divided into five chapters. The first shows the world as it existed in 1450. The following chapters tell the story of the history of the different regions of the world, while feature pages illustrate particular points of interest, such as the development of printing, the role of women, slavery, and the growth of science. Difficult words or terms, which are in **bold** in the text, can be found in the Glossary, while the Timeline at the end of the book gives an overview of the whole period.

Exploration and Empire

Old and new

Today we live in a world of fast travel and instant communication. But in 1450 most people never traveled farther than their own town or village. Others did not know that countries existed beyond their own. Great **civilizations** rose and flourished almost independently of each other.

Western Europe, which influences so much of our lives today, was on the edge of the civilized world in 1450. All around the world, civilizations such as the Mughal **Empire** in India, the Ming **Dynasty** in China, and the brilliant Aztec and Inca Empires in central and south America flourished. In west Africa the Kingdom of Benin rose to its height and in Australia the Aboriginal **culture** continued to flourish as it had done for many thousands of years, independent of any contact with the outside world.

Toward one world

But the world was poised on the brink of great change. Between 1450 and 1750 European seafarers, traders, and **colonists** set out to explore and exploit the rest of the world. This brought the continents into direct contact with each other for the first time. From 1450 the history of the world begins to move from

continued on p.10

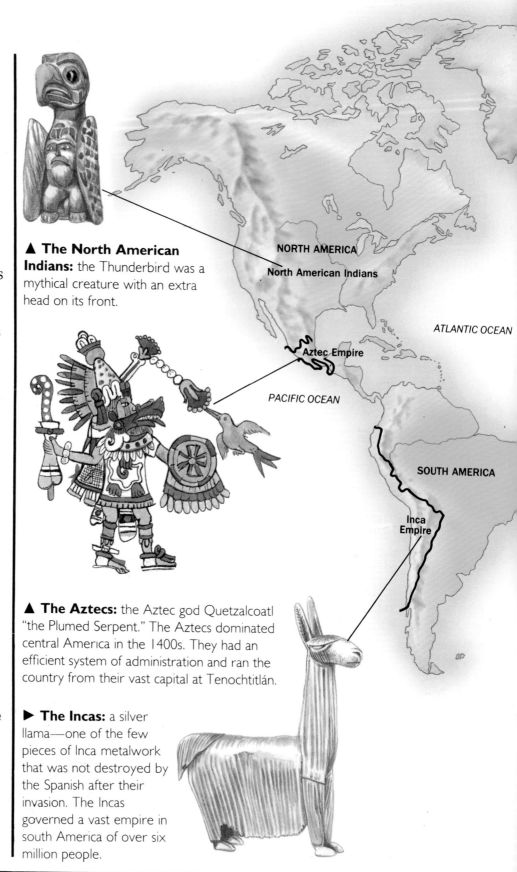

▲ **The North American Indians:** the Thunderbird was a mythical creature with an extra head on its front.

▲ **The Aztecs:** the Aztec god Quetzalcoatl "the Plumed Serpent." The Aztecs dominated central America in the 1400s. They had an efficient system of administration and ran the country from their vast capital at Tenochtitlán.

▶ **The Incas:** a silver llama—one of the few pieces of Inca metalwork that was not destroyed by the Spanish after their invasion. The Incas governed a vast empire in south America of over six million people.

NORTH AMERICA
North American Indians

ATLANTIC OCEAN

Aztec Empire

PACIFIC OCEAN

SOUTH AMERICA

Inca Empire

1450

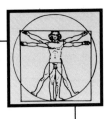

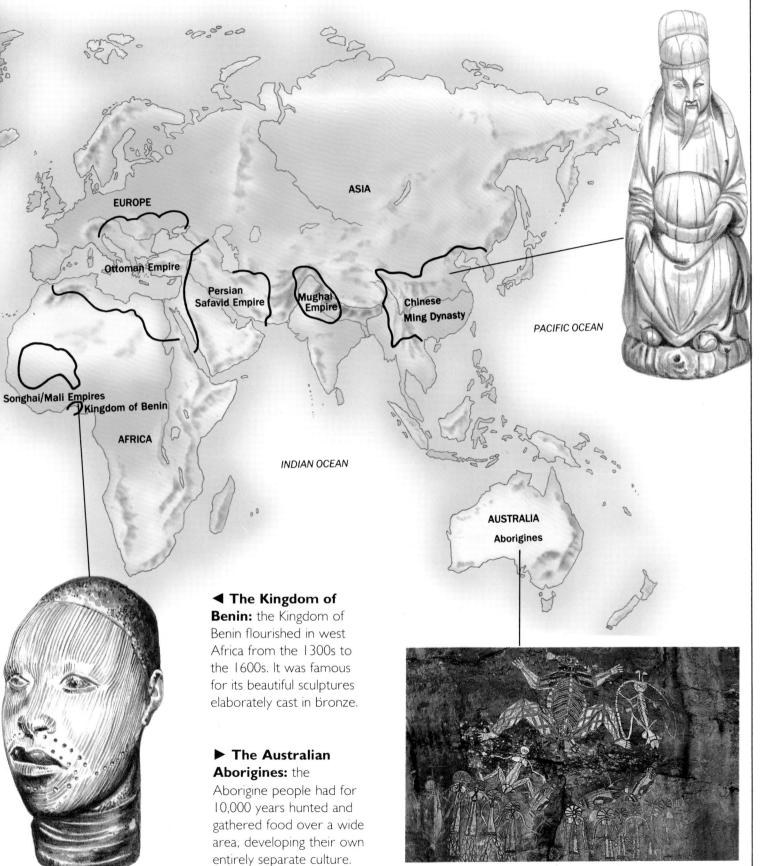

▶ **The Ming Dynasty:** an official of the Ming Dynasty finely carved in ivory. The Ming Dynasty ruled China from 1368 to 1644, creating a rich and powerful state.

ASIA

EUROPE

Ottoman Empire

Persian
Safavid Empire

Mughal
Empire

Chinese
Ming Dynasty

PACIFIC OCEAN

Songhai/Mali Empires
Kingdom of Benin

AFRICA

INDIAN OCEAN

AUSTRALIA
Aborigines

◀ **The Kingdom of Benin:** the Kingdom of Benin flourished in west Africa from the 1300s to the 1600s. It was famous for its beautiful sculptures elaborately cast in bronze.

▶ **The Australian Aborigines:** the Aborigine people had for 10,000 years hunted and gathered food over a wide area, developing their own entirely separate culture.

9

being the story of different civilizations to the history of one, interconnected world.

New ways of thinking

As we have seen, Europe in 1450 was not the richest or the most important region of the world. But it was a place where important changes were occurring. During the 1400s and 1500s there were great advances in the arts and sciences, and the beginnings of new and exciting ways of thinking about the world and human nature.

This period in European history is called the **Renaissance** (meaning *rebirth*). It began in northern Italy where wealthy and educated people began to take a renewed interest in the art and literature of Ancient Greece and Rome. This led to great artistic achievements by people such as Michelangelo, Raphael, and Leonardo da Vinci. It also stimulated interest in learning and a new spirit of inquiry, influenced by ideas from the Islamic world. The science of astronomy was developed, and there were advances in medicine. Scholars and thinkers began to challenge the rigid teaching of the medieval Church.

Helped by the invention of printing, the ideas and scholarship of the Renaissance gradually spread throughout Europe. The Renaissance only affected the wealthiest and most privileged in society but it provided a stimulus to the European urge to explore and discover the world outside.

▶ The Renaissance started among the many city-states of northern Italy. Here, art and architecture were paid for by wealthy and educated people, including women like Isabella d'Este (*below*) who took a personal interest in the new learning.

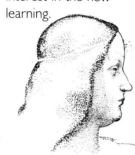

◀ Leonardo da Vinci was a painter, sculptor, architect, and engineer. Among his many drawings was an idea for a flying machine, devised 400 years before the first aircraft, and this parachute.

The Invention of Printing

Today we take newspapers and books for granted. But until the 1450s information was either passed from one person to another by word of mouth or copied and written out laboriously by hand. In the 1450s a German craftsman, Johannes Gutenberg, introduced the printing press into Europe. It revolutionized communication. For the first time books or "broadsheets" could be produced quickly and easily, which meant that more people than ever before had access to learning and ideas.

The Bible and classical texts were the first books to be printed in Europe. By 1520, there were more than 200 different printed editions of the Bible in several different languages. Printing was also used to spread the new scientific and political ideas of the Renaissance.

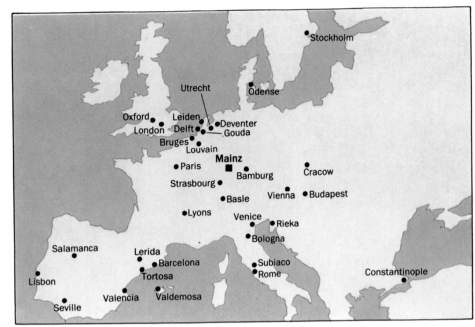

▼ Gutenberg's press, which was adapted from a wine press of the time, used movable metal type for the first time. Earlier printers carved groups of letters onto a woodblock; but individual letters cast in molds could be moved and used over and over again. The type was inked, and then separate sheets of paper, one at a time, were placed on top of the wet type. In this way whole books could be reproduced thousands of times.

▲ The first European printing press was set up, by Gutenberg, in Mainz in what is now Germany in 1454. Over the next 50 years printing presses were introduced into Germany, Italy, France, Spain, and England.

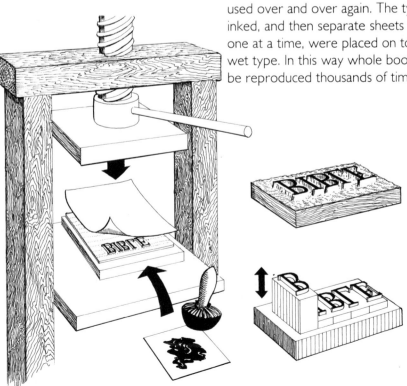

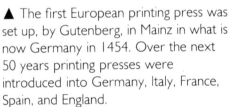

▲ The *Ladies Mercury*, one of the early broadsheets, which was printed and distributed widely.

Exploration and the Scramble for Riches

From around 1450, European sailors and navigators set out on remarkable voyages of exploration. Curiosity was one reason, the search for trade and wealth was another.

Overland trade routes had existed between Europe and Asia for centuries, along which merchants had brought spices, silks, and gems from the East to Europe. But in 1453 when the Ottoman Turks captured Constantinople (Istanbul) direct land links between Europe and Asia were cut completely. It became essential to find a sea route to the East.

In the 1460s the Portuguese explored the west coast of Africa, setting up forts and trading in gold, ivory, and silver. In 1488 Bartolomeu Dias reached the Cape of Good Hope. In 1498 Vasco da Gama was the first European to reach India by sea.

A "new world"

While the Portuguese were sailing east, the Spanish were exploring the oceans to the west. In 1492 Christopher Columbus set off to find India by sailing west. He "discovered" the Caribbean islands and, believing them to be part of Asia, called them the West Indies. He went on to find South America, part of an entire continent unknown to the Europeans.

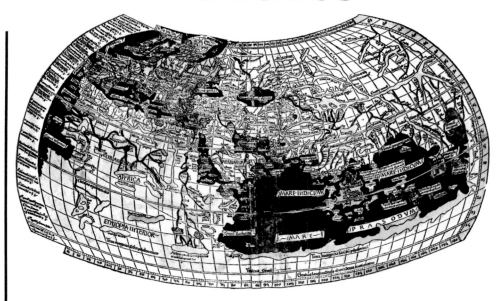

▲ Claudius Ptolemy drew his map of the world in the A.D. 100s and it was rediscovered by Europeans in the 1400s. Using this map, the first Europeans to reach America believed that it must be part of Asia because the new continent was not on the map.

▶ The European exploration of the world was made possible by a new and faster type of ship, the *caravel*, developed by the Portuguese. Nevertheless, sailing into the unknown was a frightening experience, and many of the sailors believed that monsters would threaten them while at sea.

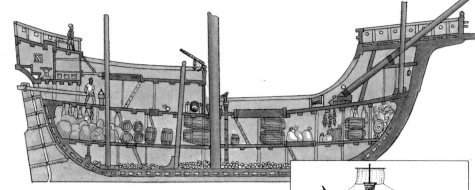

▲ Columbus's ship, the *Santa Maria*. Life aboard the *Santa Maria* was very tough—there was no sleeping accommodation for the crew and their food was cooked in an open pot on deck.

Amerigo Vespucci explored the South American coast down to the mouth of the Amazon. The previously unnamed continent in the **"New World"** was called America after him.

Between 1519 and 1522 **Ferdinand Magellan** proved that the world's oceans were linked by sailing around the world—but only 18 of his crew of 250 survived the voyage.

In 1498 **Vasco da Gama** became the first European to sail to India, in a voyage that took him around the coast of Africa.

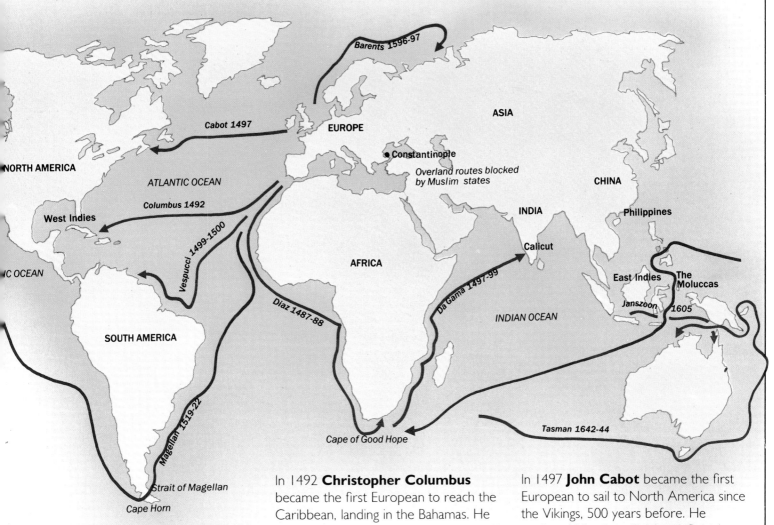

In 1492 **Christopher Columbus** became the first European to reach the Caribbean, landing in the Bahamas. He later explored the South American coast.

In 1497 **John Cabot** became the first European to sail to North America since the Vikings, 500 years before. He explored Newfoundland and Canada.

Cheng Ho

Almost a century before the Europeans sailed into the Indian Ocean, the Chinese Ming rulers sent seven expeditions to explore this area. Commanded by Cheng Ho, vast fleets explored as far afield as east Africa, the Red Sea, Persia, India, and Java. They brought back gifts from the local rulers, rare spices, and unusual animals, including lions and giraffes.

Compass **Astrolabe** **Backstaff**

▲ Navigation at sea was a very primitive affair in the 1500s. The most important instrument was the compass which told which direction the ship was sailing in. The **astrolabe** and backstaff used the Sun to calculate the ship's distance north or south of the Equator. Sailors had no accurate way of finding out how far east or west they were until the mid-1700s.

1450–1650

Gold, guns, and disease

Explorers and navigators were followed by **conquistadors** and colonists in search of land and gold for their countries. The Spanish first occupied the Caribbean and then turned their attention to South and Central America, which were rich in gold and silver.

When the Spanish arrived in Central and South America they found two great civilizations—the Aztecs of Mexico and the Incas of Peru. Both were highly organized societies of millions of people. The Aztecs had developed astronomy, methods of **irrigation**, and a highly diverse agriculture, growing crops such as corn, tobacco, potatoes, and tomatoes which the Europeans later took back to Europe. Both Aztecs and Incas were highly skilled builders. Tenochtitlán, the Aztec capital which lay on Lake Texcoco, was larger than any European city of the time. Yet between 1519 and 1534 both empires were overthrown by the Spanish and their wealth and land seized.

The Spanish conquest was achieved by Hernán Cortés who overthrew Aztec rule between 1519 and 1521, and by Francisco Pizarro who conquered the Inca Empire between 1532 and 1534. Although the Spanish were few in number they brought guns and horses against which the American peoples had no defense. As a result the Spanish were able to capture the Aztec and Inca leaders very easily.

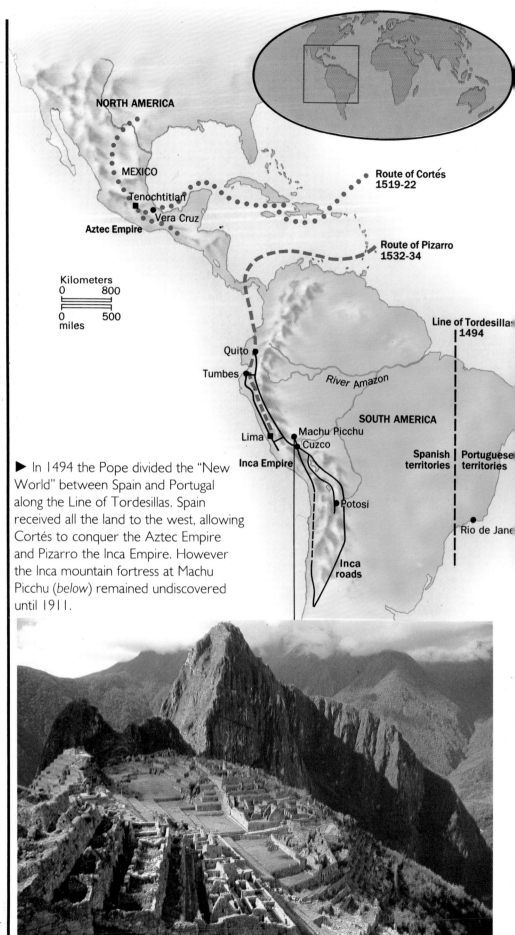

▶ In 1494 the Pope divided the "New World" between Spain and Portugal along the Line of Tordesillas. Spain received all the land to the west, allowing Cortés to conquer the Aztec Empire and Pizarro the Inca Empire. However the Inca mountain fortress at Machu Picchu (*below*) remained undiscovered until 1911.

▲ In order to exploit the gold and silver of the "New World," the Spanish put the native Americans to work in the mines. Conditions were harsh and many thousands died.

► When the first Europeans arrived in the Aztec Empire in 1519, its ruler Montezuma believed them to be gods and welcomed them into the capital, showering them with gifts.

◄ This snake, made of hollow wood covered with turquoise, was made by Aztec craftspeople and probably sent as a tribute to Tenochtitlán. It was worn at the back of the head as part of a headdress.

When the Spanish began to conquer South America in 1519, the native population was about 57 million. By 1607, this had dropped to just over 4 million. Some of this decline was due to warfare and harsh conditions in the mines, but much of it was because of the introduction of European diseases, such as measles, smallpox, and chickenpox, against which the native peoples had no **immunity**.

▼ The central part of the great Aztec city, Tenochtitlán. The city was begun in 1325 and built on an island on Lake Texcoco.

Temple of Huitzilopochtli

Priests' quarters

Sacrificial skull-rack

Temple of the Sun

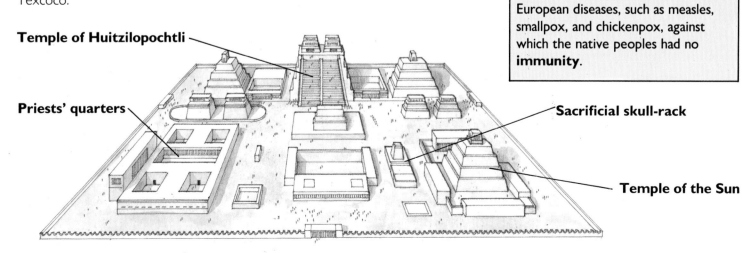

The scramble for riches

By the mid-1550s the Spanish and Portuguese had established the first European overseas empires. They set up **plantations** in the Caribbean and colonized large areas of South America. In 1510 the Portuguese captured Goa in India. In the 1540s they became the first Europeans to land in Japan. By the 1550s they controlled trade in the Indian Ocean and the **Spice Islands**. But from the late 1500s onward **The Netherlands**, France, and England began to challenge Spain and Portugal and to compete with them for trade, in spices and slaves.

England was already a great sea power and trading nation. As well as trading for slaves in the Caribbean, English pirates and sailors such as Francis Drake raided the Spanish colonies in the Americas, plundering their ships and carrying off gold, silver, and other treasure. In 1588 Philip the Second of Spain sent an armed fleet—the **Armada**—to attack England, but the Spanish fleet failed in its task. This weakened Spain's empire and led to the growth of British power overseas.

The Dutch too were a prosperous nation. They drove the Portuguese out of the Spice Islands and in 1658 they captured Ceylon (Sri Lanka). By the 1680s they had built up their own empire in Southeast Asia. By 1650 the European nations had established a sea-trading network that stretched as far as India.

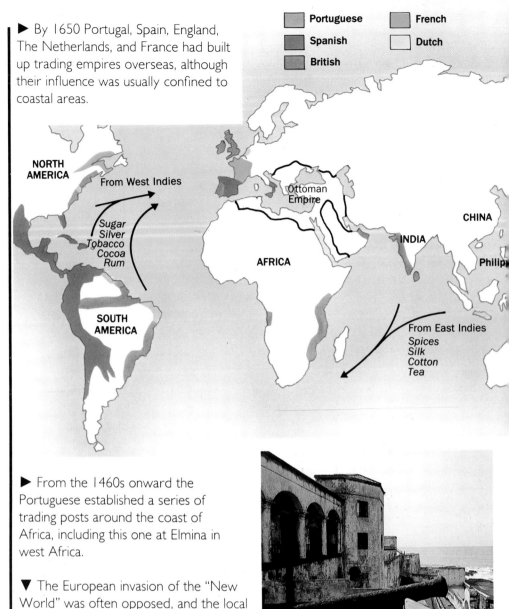

▶ By 1650 Portugal, Spain, England, The Netherlands, and France had built up trading empires overseas, although their influence was usually confined to coastal areas.

Portuguese	French
Spanish	Dutch
British	

▶ From the 1460s onward the Portuguese established a series of trading posts around the coast of Africa, including this one at Elmina in west Africa.

▼ The European invasion of the "New World" was often opposed, and the local peoples continued to fight the invaders for years. In 1608 the **Caribs** of St. Lucia fought against the British colonists.

The Spice Trade

When the Portuguese reached the East Indies in the early 1500s, they found the islands rich in spices unobtainable in Europe. The Portuguese quickly took control of this lucrative trade by conquering the Moluccas and seizing the main ports in the Indian Ocean and China through which the spice trade passed.

For almost a century, the Portuguese controlled the spice trade with Europe, but by 1600, both England and The Netherlands had established East India Companies to obtain spices directly for themselves. The Dutch were the most successful, driving the Portuguese out of the Moluccas and keeping the English out of the region altogether. They encouraged the growing of tea, coffee, sugar, and tobacco on the islands, and by 1720 they had become the main coffee suppliers to Europe.

▲ Harvesting pepper cloves in the Spice Islands.

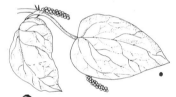

▲ Pepper is used to season food and flavor soups and gravies.

▲ Nutmeg is used to flavor custards and milk puddings.

▲ Cloves are used to flavor food, particularly meat.

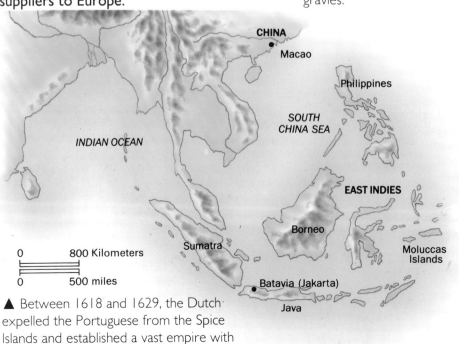

▲ Between 1618 and 1629, the Dutch expelled the Portuguese from the Spice Islands and established a vast empire with its capital at Batavia (Jakarta).

▲ Mace is used in pickles and hot mulled wines.

Religion and Change

In the early 1500s the Christian Roman Catholic Church was the main religion in Europe. The Church was the most powerful force in society: it dominated people's thinking. But within 50 years, almost half the population of western Europe had left the Roman Catholic Church to worship in rival Christian Churches. This change is called the Reformation. It resulted from a protest about the corruption of the Roman Catholic Church and its priests, and a demand for reform.

In 1517 a German monk called Martin Luther wrote a list of 95 "theses," or complaints, which were printed and circulated throughout Europe. The Church refused to consider reform and Luther was **excommunicated**, or expelled, from the Roman Catholic Church in 1520. Luther then set up his own reformed Church in Saxony. Similar Churches were soon established in the rest of Germany and northern Europe.

In order to regain control of Europe, in 1545 the Roman Catholic Church began to reform itself, in a movement called the Counter-Reformation. The Counter-Reformation led to bitter civil wars, and a general European war that lasted 30 years from 1618 to 1648.

Europe in 1560

Roman Catholic

Protestant

SCOTLAND
SWEDEN
IRELAND
ENGLAND
POLAND
Wittenberg
SAXONY
Paris
FRANCE
Worms
SWISS CANTONS
HUNGARY
Geneva
Genoa
OTTOMAN EMPIRE Muslim
PORTUGAL
Rome
SPAIN

Boundary between Ror Catholic and Greek and Russian Ortl churches

▲ By 1560 the people of Europe were divided by their religion. Those who broke away from the power of the Roman Catholic Church are shown as Protestants on the map—in fact there were many different new movements, the Anglicans in England, the New Lutherans, and the Calvinists for example. In the east the Russian and Greek Orthodox Christian Churches had long been established, and in the southeast, the Ottoman Empire was Muslim in faith.

▶ Martin Luther. His followers were called Protestants because they protested against the Roman Catholic Church.

▼ Inside St. Peter's in Rome, the center of the Roman Catholic Church.

◄ The Calvinist Church was based on the severe and strict teachings of John Calvin, a Frenchman living in Geneva. Its buildings were stark in comparison with the decorative Roman Catholic churches.

▼ From 1562 to 1598, France was split by religious wars between Roman Catholics and Huguenots, or Protestants of the Calvinist Church. The Roman Catholic Queen, Catherine de Medici, ordered all the Huguenots to be killed on St. Bartholomew's Day in 1572. Over 29,000 were murdered.

Henry the Eighth of England
In England, Henry the Eighth wanted to divorce his wife, Catherine of Aragon, because she had failed to produce a male heir to the throne. The Roman Catholic Church would not agree, so Henry made himself head of the new Anglican Church and granted his own divorce. He dissolved the monasteries, the richest landowners in the country, and seized their wealth, increasing his own power.

19

Rich and poor

In the 1500s and 1600s in Europe the vast majority of people lived off the land. Famine, poverty, and disease were common and few people lived past the age of 40. Most remained poor and uneducated, lacking the knowledge or equipment to farm efficiently. The weather and harvest were the most crucial aspects of their lives.

But changes were taking place that gradually altered people's lives. Between 1500 and 1700 the population of Europe grew steadily, leading to pressure for more efficient and productive farming. In some countries, such as England, wealthy local landowners began to enclose open fields and **common land** in order to make higher profits: they turned **arable** land into **pasture** for sheep, and threw the peasant farmers off the land.

In the towns, rich merchants were profiting from increased trade and **commerce** throughout Europe and with the rest of the world. With their new-found wealth they invested their money in the new banks set up to finance the growing **merchant economy**. Many rich people were also commissioning fine buildings and works of art, particularly in The Netherlands, which by 1650 was the richest country in Europe. The growth of the new merchant class, dedicated to business and profit, meant that by 1650 the gap between rich and poor had become very wide.

▲ The first plows had a single wedge, tipped with iron, that could only break the surface of the soil, not turn it. By the middle of the 1600s double plows were in use throughout Europe. These new plows were able to turn the soil and to prepare it better for planting the crops.

▼ Most people who lived in the 1500s and 1600s were poor, living on the land and dependent on a good harvest for their livelihood. This painting by Breughel shows the living room of a Flemish farmer in the early 1600s. A rich nobleman and his wife bring presents of salt and money to the farmer's family.

The Potato
In 1500, the potato grew in the Andes mountains of South America and the only people who ate it were the Incas. Their Spanish conquerors introduced it into Europe in the middle of the 1500s, but it was about 200 years before it became the popular food in Europe that it is today. In about 1600, the potato was taken back across the Atlantic by settlers who introduced it to North America.

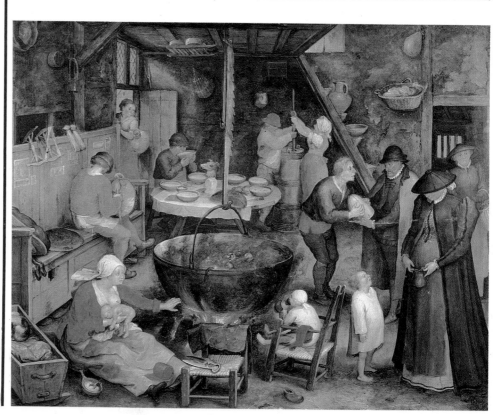

Nuns, Witches, and Dissenters

▲ The Quakers were a religious group which began in the mid-1600s in England. They were also known as the Society of Friends. They believed that men and women were equal – this picture shows a woman preaching at a meeting.

Life was hard for most women during this period because by law women had few rights. Their lives and their fortunes were controlled by their fathers or, if they were married, by their husbands. Most women worked in the fields and brought up many children.

Some unmarried women entered convents as nuns. In 1535 one nun, Angela Merici, founded a teaching order, the Ursulines who later emigrated to North America and set up the first convent in Quebec in 1639. Other older women were herbalists or wise women who tended the sick in the villages. Many people were very suspicious of these women, who suffered and were persecuted as witches during the 1400s and 1500s.

Women also played some part in the political and social changes of the time. In Italy and France a number of notable women, such as Lucrezia Borgia and the artist Artesemia Gemileschi, played a leading role in the new learning. By the 1600s, some women were beginning to demand women's rights. In England during a time of political and religious dissent in the 1640s a pamphlet appeared. It was called *The Women's Sharpe Revenge*. Written by two women who called themselves Mary Tattle-well and Joan Hit-him-home, it attacked the critics of women and was an early demand for women's rights.

▼ In Europe in the 1400s and 1500s, thousands of women were accused of being witches and tortured and burned as a result.

▼ Noblewomen did have certain traditional rights in the 1400s and 1500s, but from the 1600s onward these were gradually taken away. Lady Anne Clifford was an English noblewoman who fought against the loss of these rights.

The Ottoman Empire

To the east of Europe lay one of the largest and most successful empires in the world—the Ottoman Empire. It had been founded by Muslim Turks in the late 1200s. Under their king, Osman the First, from whom the empire took its name, the Ottomans managed to exploit the weaknesses and divisions of their neighbors and establish dominance over Anatolia (Turkey) and then farther afield in Europe, Asia, and Africa. Their greatest triumph came in 1453 when they captured the great Christian city of Constantinople, capital of the Byzantine Empire.

They renamed this city Istanbul and made it the capital of their vast empire. At its greatest extent in 1566, the Ottoman Empire covered almost a million square miles, from Algeria to Arabia and from Budapest to Cairo. In 1529 and again in 1683, the Ottomans even reached the capital of the Holy Roman Empire, Vienna, in the heart of Europe, but were unable to capture it.

Throughout most of the 1500s, the Ottoman Empire was at war with its neighbor, the Safavid Empire of Persia (Iran). Like Christian Europe, the Muslim world was divided, for while the Ottomans were of the Sunni sect, the Safavids were Shi'ites, and the two sects fought many wars on religious grounds. This dispute still continues today.

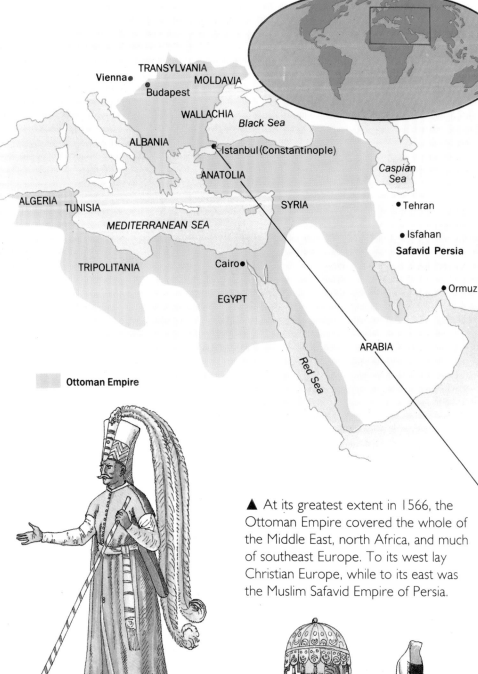

▲ At its greatest extent in 1566, the Ottoman Empire covered the whole of the Middle East, north Africa, and much of southeast Europe. To its west lay Christian Europe, while to its east was the Muslim Safavid Empire of Persia.

In order to fight their many wars, the Ottomans had a highly-trained army led by Janissaries (*above*). Distinguished by their tall plumed hats, these élite troops were Christians, captured or recruited from Europe. Ottoman women, however, were considered little better than the servants employed by each rich household. This Turkish lady and her servant are on the way to the baths (*right*).

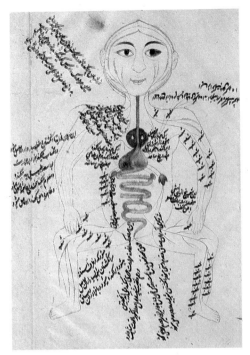

▲ The study of medicine was very advanced in the Islamic world. This Persian manuscript of the 1600s shows an understanding of the human organs and the circulation of the blood.

▶ Suleiman brought Ottoman power to its peak when he brought his armies to the gates of Vienna. He is seen here at the Battle of Mohács in 1526, when he defeated the Hungarian army. *Upper center:* Suleiman rides his horse through a pile of dead bodies. *Lower corner:* defeated Hungarians flee on horseback.

After the capture of Constantinople in 1453, the Ottomans renamed the city Istanbul and made it their capital. Minarets were built on to the Christian church of St. Sophia and it was turned into a mosque (*below and left*).

The Mughal Empire

At the same time as the Ottoman Turks and the Persian Safavids were establishing their empires, a third empire was being founded in India. All three were Islamic. Together they ensured that by the 1500s the Islamic world was far larger than the Christian.

The Islamic empire in India was founded in 1504 when a group of Turks led by Babur captured Kabul in Afghanistan. Babur claimed descent from the Mongol ruler Genghis Khan; from the word Mongol came Mughal. Babur soon moved south into the fertile plains of northern India and in 1526 his army of 12,000 defeated a 100,000-strong Indian army. Establishing their capital at Delhi, Babur and his successors spread Mughal rule over most of India by the mid-1600s.

Although the Mughals were Muslims, four-fifths of their subjects were Hindus who were at first allowed to practice their religion unhindered. But by the 1700s the Hindus were being persecuted, leading to strains within the Empire that eventually led to its break-up.

A further threat came from the fact that the Mughals had never had much interest in the sea or overseas trade, allowing Europeans, notably the Portuguese, to establish trading ports around the coast as early as 1510. These ports soon developed into bases for European powers seeking to expand their own trading and colonial empires abroad.

▲ In 1650, at the height of its power, the Mughal Empire covered almost all of present-day India, Pakistan, and Bangladesh. Many of its coastal towns were occupied by Europeans, notably the Portuguese, Dutch, French, and English.

▲ Although the Mughals were Muslims, they tolerated other religions within their empire, notably the Sikhs. The Golden Temple in the city of Amritsar is the holiest shrine of the Sikh religion.

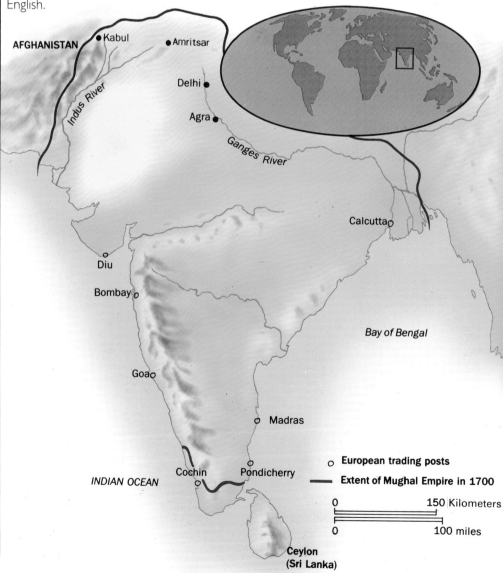

European trading posts

Extent of Mughal Empire in 1700

0   150 Kilometers

0   100 miles

The first European settlements in India were founded not by countries but by trading companies, such as the British East India Company. Set up in 1600 with a charter from Elizabeth I of England to trade with the East, it soon acquired many privileges from the Mughals, employing local women (*above*) to produce cotton for export and planting large estates with tea (*right*) to satisfy the British thirst for the drink.

▼ When Babur became Mughal Emperor, he complained that India had no grapes, good fruits, or cold water. He therefore encouraged the building of beautiful gardens.

▼ Built as a mausoleum (tomb) for Mumtaz, the favorite wife of Emperor Shah Jahan, the Taj Mahal took 20,000 builders 18 years to complete. It was finally ready in 1648.

Slavery and the New World

A hundred years or so after Columbus arrived in the Americas, people from all over Europe began to cross the Atlantic to settle in what they called the "New World." The Portuguese and Spanish concentrated on Central and South America and the Caribbean. There they mined for silver and set up vast plantations which were worked by slave labor, growing profitable crops, such as tobacco, sugar, and cotton.

The French, Dutch, and British concentrated on North America. In 1535 the Frenchman, Jacques Cartier, sailed up the St. Lawrence River and established a port at Montreal in what is now Canada. French influence then extended into central North America, which the French called Louisiana after their king, Louis the Fourteenth.

In 1607 the British set up their first American colony at Jamestown in Virginia. They continued to colonize the Atlantic coast, expelling the Dutch from New York in 1664, and by 1700 more than 250,000 English people were living in North America. They organized their settlements into 12 colonies, a thirteenth, Georgia, being formed in 1732. These 13 colonies eventually formed the first states of the United States of America.

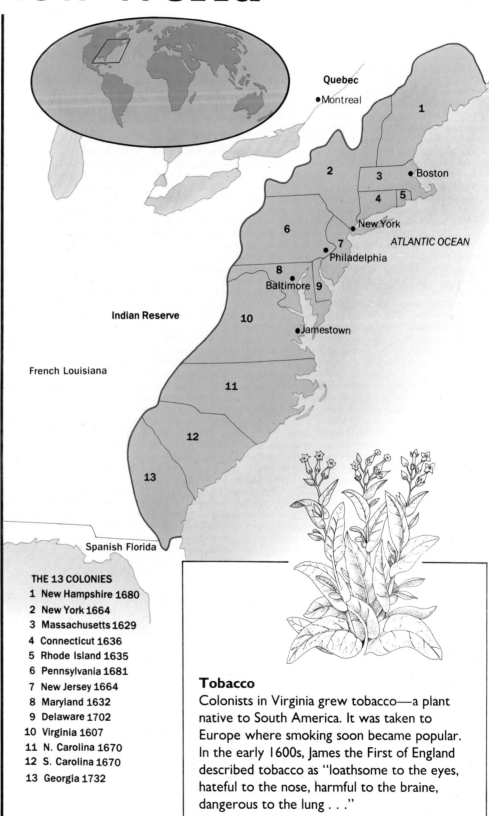

THE 13 COLONIES
1 New Hampshire 1680
2 New York 1664
3 Massachusetts 1629
4 Connecticut 1636
5 Rhode Island 1635
6 Pennsylvania 1681
7 New Jersey 1664
8 Maryland 1632
9 Delaware 1702
10 Virginia 1607
11 N. Carolina 1670
12 S. Carolina 1670
13 Georgia 1732

Tobacco
Colonists in Virginia grew tobacco—a plant native to South America. It was taken to Europe where smoking soon became popular. In the early 1600s, James the First of England described tobacco as "loathsome to the eyes, hateful to the nose, harmful to the braine, dangerous to the lung . . ."

▲ The native tribes of North America lived by hunting and trapping wild animals for their fur and meat. In this picture the native Americans camouflage themselves in order to stalk their prey. At first this way of life was unaffected by the arrival of the Europeans. But gradually the two groups came into bitter conflict as the native Americans were driven from their land by the expanding European colonies.

▶ One of the first settlers in North America was John White, a map-maker and artist, who drew pictures of the native Americans, including this one of a woman and her child.

Many of the first European colonists were dissenters, people who disagreed with the accepted religion in their country, and who were persecuted for their beliefs. One of these groups, the Pilgrim Fathers, was made up of Puritan men and women who disagreed with the English Anglican Church. They left England in 1620 on the *Mayflower* (*above*) and founded a settlement in Massachusetts.

A PURITAN FAMILY.

Settlers and Americans

The early European settlers found existing cultures already established on their arrival in the "New World." At that time North America contained many different tribes of native Americans, each with their own customs and ways of life. The first settlers met with little opposition, as their small numbers posed no threat to the local inhabitants, whom they named "Indians." The settlers needed the Indians to supply them with food and furs to supplement the unreliable deliveries from Europe and to help them through the harsh winters and years of crop failure. At the same time, the Indians wanted to acquire arms to fight their local wars.

Local **alliances** soon sprang up, and in Canada, the French helped one Indian tribe, the Iroquois, to destroy another, the Huron, in 1649, while farther south similar alliances were forged between the British settlers and local Indian groups. These alliances divided the Indians and prevented a united Indian threat to the fledgling colonies.

But as the European colonies grew, they began to threaten the livelihood and independence of the Indians. The British colonists in Connecticut were attacked by the Pequot Indians in 1637, while all the New England colonies were involved in a war against the Wampanoag and Narragansett Indians in 1675–6, which led to the virtual destruction of tribal life in the area.

▲ The first European settlers built themselves simple log cabins able to withstand the cold winters they encountered in the "New World." But as they established themselves, they cleared more land and built bigger and more comfortable houses.

▼ The native Americans were experienced in trapping wild animals, especially beavers, for their skin and fur, which they traded with the European settlers for arms and other goods.

▼ In 1612 the Dutch settled on an island in the Hudson River and named the place New Amsterdam. When the English captured it in 1664, they renamed it New York. This map was drawn in 1664 and shows the English fleet in the harbor.

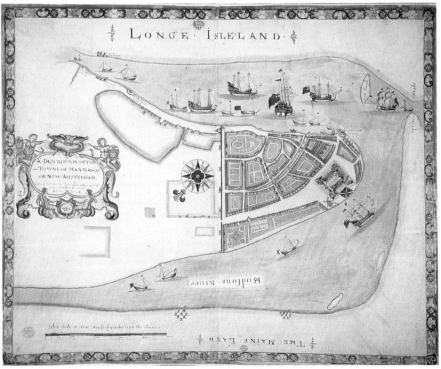

The Slave Trade

Between the 1400s and 1800s at least 10 million black Africans were shipped from Africa to labor on the sugar, tobacco, and cotton plantations of the Caribbean and North America. The Portuguese were the first to practice this trade in human lives; later the British became the main slave traders. In a horrendous but profitable **"triangular trade"** ships sailed from Britain with manufactured goods which were exchanged for slaves on the west coast of Africa. Cargoes of slaves—women, men, and children—were taken across the Atlantic (the "middle passage") and then sold in the Caribbean and North and South America where most were worked to death on the plantations. The same ships then took the products of the plantations—cotton, raw sugar (known as white gold because it was so profitable), and tobacco—back to Europe where they were sold.

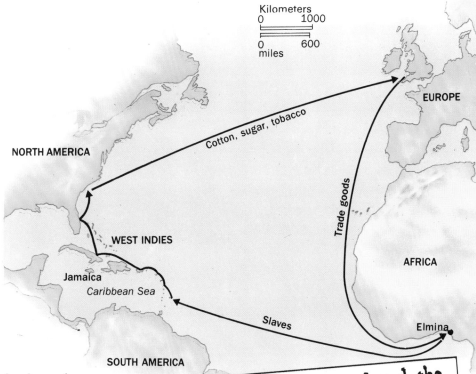

Kilometers
0   1000
0   600
miles

EUROPE

NORTH AMERICA

Cotton, sugar, tobacco

Trade goods

WEST INDIES

AFRICA

Jamaica
Caribbean Sea

Slaves

Elmina

SOUTH AMERICA

◀ Many black Africans rebelled. The fighting **Maroons** of Jamaica were a colony of escaped slaves who, in 1739, forced the British to make a **treaty** with them.

▼ During the middle passage from Africa to the Americas hundreds of black Africans were crammed together on disease-ridden slave ships and transported across the Atlantic in appalling conditions. Many perished.

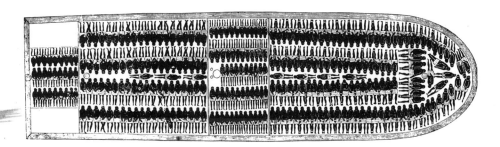

TO BE SOLD on board the Ship *Bance-Ifland*, on tuefday the 6th of *May* next, at *Afhley-Ferry*; a choice cargo of about 250 fine healthy NEGROES, juft arrived from the Windward & Rice Coaft. —The utmoft care has already been taken, and fhall be continued, to keep them free from the leaft danger of being infected with the SMALL-POX, no boat having been on board, and all other communication with people from *Charles-Town* prevented.
Auftin, Laurens, & Appleby.

N. B. Full one Half of the above Negroes have had the SMALL-POX in their own Country.

Africa

By the 1500s the African continent was home to many different political **states** and powerful kingdoms. Within the continent these societies had developed trade networks, advanced forms of agriculture, gold mining, cloth working, and a variety of crafts and skills. Contact between these states and the rest of the world was limited, for the Sahara Desert was an almost impassable barrier to all but the hardiest of traders. But the gradual spread of Islam across the desert linked Africa more closely to the Arab world and by the 1600s trade between Africa and the Mediterranean was well established.

The slave trade

The arrival of the Europeans interrupted African development. At first European settlement was limited to coastal areas as the Portuguese began to trade with west African kings for gold, ivory, pepper, and cloth in exchange for goods, most of which were of little use to the Africans. Slaves also formed part of this trade. At first, European demand for slaves was met by west African states where slavery existed as punishment for various crimes. But by the 1700s Europeans were buying or kidnapping slaves from the whole of Africa. The effect on African cultures was devastating and by the late 1700s the population had declined and many African states were seriously weakened.

BRANDING SLAVES,
ON THE COAST OF AFRICA PREVIOUS TO EMBARKATION.

▲ When a slave was captured, he or she was branded, as described in a contemporary French account, "with a red-hot iron, imprinting the mark of the French, English, or Dutch companies, so that each nation may distinguish its own. Care is taken that the women, as tenderest, be not burnt too hard."

► An ivory carving from west Africa depicting Portuguese soldiers in a miniature ship's crow's nest.

▼ Built on an island off Tanzania, the town of Kilwa became the major trading port in east Africa in the 1200s, "with many fair houses of stone and mortar, surrounded by orchards and fruit gardens irrigated by fresh water." In 1505 the Portuguese captured the town and built a fort to control it.

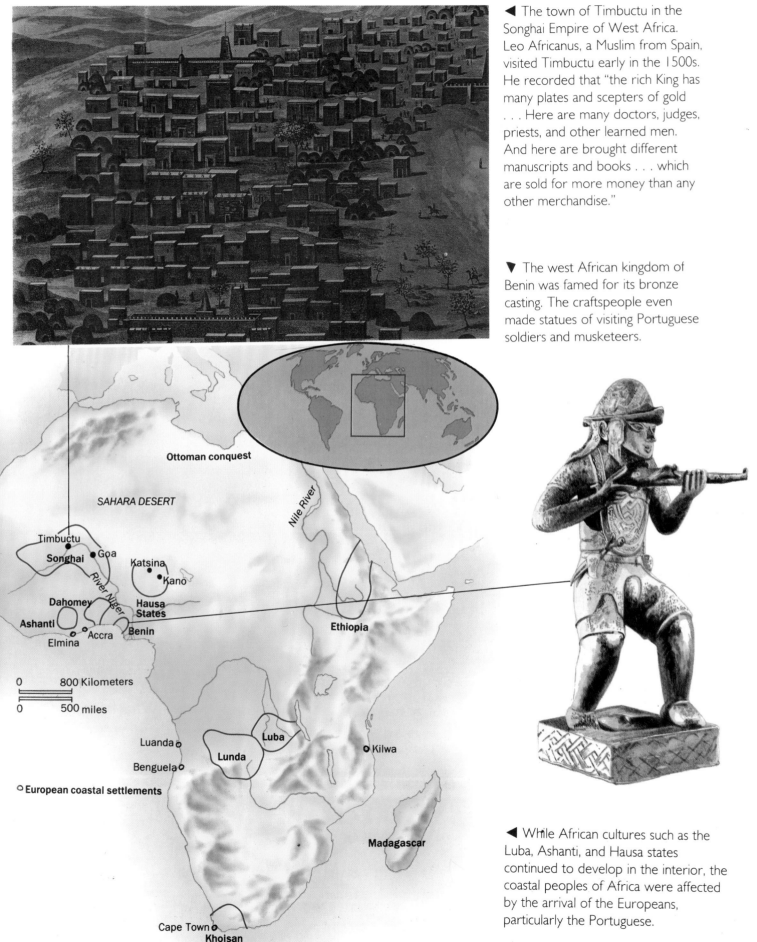

◀ The town of Timbuctu in the Songhai Empire of West Africa. Leo Africanus, a Muslim from Spain, visited Timbuctu early in the 1500s. He recorded that "the rich King has many plates and scepters of gold . . . Here are many doctors, judges, priests, and other learned men. And here are brought different manuscripts and books . . . which are sold for more money than any other merchandise."

▼ The west African kingdom of Benin was famed for its bronze casting. The craftspeople even made statues of visiting Portuguese soldiers and musketeers.

Ottoman conquest

SAHARA DESERT

Nile River

Timbuctu
Songhai • Goa
River Niger
Katsina •
• Kano
Dahomey
Hausa States
Ashanti
Accra
Benin
Elmina

Ethiopia

0   800 Kilometers
0   500 miles

Luanda ○
Lunda
Luba
Benguela ○
○ Kilwa

○ European coastal settlements

Madagascar

Cape Town ○
Khoisan

◀ While African cultures such as the Luba, Ashanti, and Hausa states continued to develop in the interior, the coastal peoples of Africa were affected by the arrival of the Europeans, particularly the Portuguese.

Struggles for Power

In 1648, the Peace of Westphalia brought to an end the Thirty Years War between the Catholic **Habsburg** emperors and their Protestant subjects in the Holy Roman Empire. It also marked an important turning point. European wars until 1648 had been fought mainly on religious grounds. Now different nations began to struggle amongst each other for political supremacy in Europe, and for trade and colonies abroad.

Between 1667 and 1714 France was involved in four major wars. At first these wars were to secure French frontiers in the east. But in 1700, when Charles the Second, King of Spain, died, it appeared possible that either Austria or France would take over Spain — with its possessions in Italy, The Netherlands, and the Americas — and thus dominate Europe. Alliances between different European countries were formed to support the two rival claimants to the throne and this led to what is called the War of the Spanish Succession. It lasted from 1702 until 1713 and involved all the major nations of Europe. It was the first major war fought to maintain what is known as a "**balance of power**" in which no single nation has more power than another.

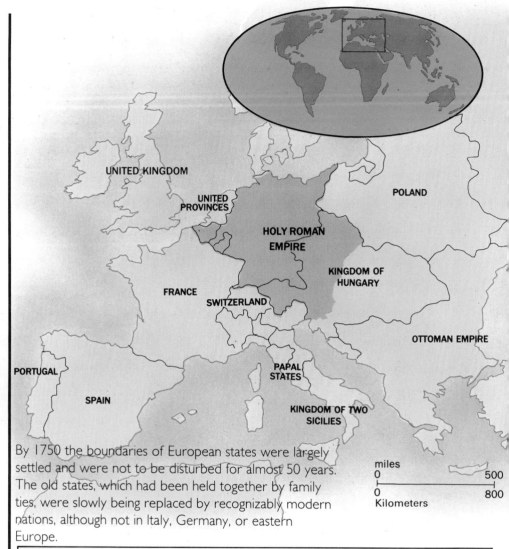

By 1750 the boundaries of European states were largely settled and were not to be disturbed for almost 50 years. The old states, which had been held together by family ties, were slowly being replaced by recognizably modern nations, although not in Italy, Germany, or eastern Europe.

The English Revolution
There were many different causes of the English **Civil War**: its origins lay in the **authoritarian** behavior of the Stuart kings, who threatened the powers of the Parliament. Religious differences were important too: the Puritans in Parliament suspected the Stuart kings of Roman Catholic sympathies. Civil War broke out in 1642 and was resolved by the execution of King Charles the First in 1649.

For the next 11 years a **republic** was set up, the only one in British history, and the country was governed, first by Parliament and then by Oliver Cromwell (*above*), an army leader. After Cromwell's death in 1658 Charles the Second returned from exile and in 1660 was reinstated, but with his royal powers considerably reduced.

The Scientific Revolution

As a result of the Renaissance and Reformation, scientists began to question the idea that all knowledge came from the Roman Catholic Church. In mathematics, physics, astronomy, and medicine new ideas were proposed, all of which could be quickly spread by the printing press. Scientists began to criticise existing theories and make their own observations.

The belief that the Earth was the center of the Universe was challenged by Copernicus in 1543, and his ideas were supported by Galileo Galilei in the next century. Both men thought that the Sun was the center of the Solar System, although few people believed them, but the explanation of how the Earth revolves daily on its axis around the Sun was not made until 1687, when Newton described the force of gravity that holds the Solar System together.

This explanation would not have been possible without the advances made in mathematics. New measuring instruments, such as the thermometer and the barometer, were invented. So too was the microscope, used by Robert Hooke to magnify animal and plant cells. In medicine, Vesalius showed the structure of the human body, while William Harvey, who first discovered the circulation of blood, showed how the body worked.

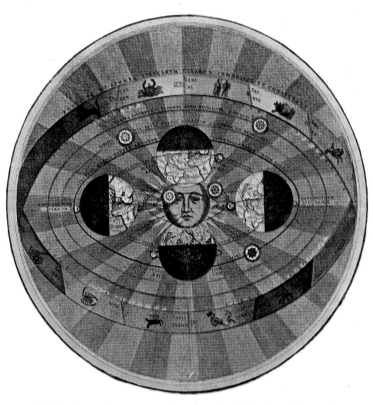

▲ The Solar System as described by Nicolaus Copernicus, a Polish scientist, in 1543. The Sun is shown at the center of the Solar System with the Earth orbiting around it.

▼ Louis the Fourteenth visits the Académie Royale des Sciences in 1671. Founded in 1666, the French Académie was a learned body that helped spread new ideas.

▲ Isaac Newton, the scientist who explained the force of gravity. He also invented a reflecting telescope and introduced a branch of mathematics called calculus.

France, the absolute state

During the 1600s and 1700s much of Europe was ruled by kings, queens, and emperors who were extremely powerful. Unlike European royal families today, these rulers were directly responsible for the economic, political, and social lives of their countries and people.

Louis the Fourteenth, ruler of France from 1643 to 1715, was the most powerful of these **absolute monarchs**. All decisions were approved by him, and power was concentrated in his hands: he once summed up his position in the words "L'état, c'est moi": *I am the state*. His absolute control was admired and copied by other European monarchs.

After a series of rebellions between 1648 and 1653 by leading nobles against the crown, France welcomed the strong rule of its king. But Louis required money for his many adventurous schemes. This was found by raising taxes and exploiting the wealth of France's colonies in Canada and the West Indies. The first great canal to be built in Europe since Roman times was constructed, while new roads and financial grants all helped to build up industry and commerce.

The wealth created was used to make the French army into the biggest in Europe and to finance the wars that Louis fought. After his death, however, further costly wars drained the country's resources and left France in a weakened conditioned.

1648–1760

▶ Under the rule of Louis the Fourteenth, the borders of France were almost the same as they are today. They were made secure against attack from the Habsburgs who ruled Spain, Italy, and the Holy Roman Empire. Inside France all opposition to Louis was crushed, and the king ruled from his palace at Versailles, near Paris.

◀ Louis the Fourteenth was the dominant ruler in Europe throughout the 1600s. He believed in Absolutism—that the king has complete control to rule his country as he wishes.

▼ At the salon of Madame Geoffrin in 1725. Groups of aristocrats met regularly to discuss art and philosophy. These salons were the only places that women could have any impact on the intellectual or political life of the day.

▼ The royal palace at Versailles was designed to glorify Louis the Fourteenth, the "Sun King." Surrounded by vast gardens and a park, the huge palace contained a Hall of Mirrors and many other sumptuously decorated state rooms. The high cost of running the palace was met by imposing taxes on the impoverished population.

▼ Plague, famine, and high taxes made many of the poor people homeless and they were forced to beg for food. The French peasants relied on the annual harvest—if the harvest failed they went hungry. Lack of food also made them more vulnerable to catching diseases such as the plague.

The Enlightenment

In almost every country in western Europe in the middle of the 1600s, an intellectual movement grew up, which became known as the Enlightenment. It questioned existing beliefs, and attempted to "throw light" on every area of human activity and thought. Its participants believed in the power of people to reason things out for themselves. Their thirst for knowledge included an interest in science and a curiosity about the peoples, plants, and animals from those parts of the world the Europeans were only just discovering for themselves.

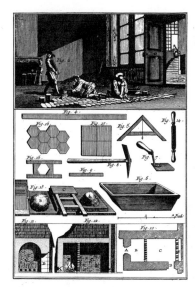

One of the main achievements was the vast Encyclopedia (*left*) of all human knowledge, compiled between 1751 and 1777 by the French **philosopher**, Diderot. Another Frenchman, Descartes, provided the philosophical basis of the movement with the saying: "I think, therefore I am."

This new thinking challenged the existing authorities, such as the Church: some scientists, such as Galileo, were imprisoned, while the books of Descartes were banned. But this questioning of authority could not be supressed and in France was one of the causes of the **French Revolution**.

The emergence of Russia

Before 1450, much of southern Russia was controlled by the Khanate of the Golden Horde, a powerful state ruled by the Mongols of central Asia, who managed to isolate Russia from European developments. But as the power of the Mongols lessened, the small region of Muscovy exerted its independence. In 1480, its ruler, Ivan the Third, declared himself "**Tsar** of all the Russias" and appointed himself protector of the Orthodox Church.

Ivan the Third rebuilt Moscow with the help of Italian architects and began to expand the Muscovite state westward. Expansion continued under successive tsars and by 1647 Russia dominated Siberia in the east but was unable to expand any farther toward Europe because of Polish and Swedish power.

In 1682 Peter the Great became Tsar of Russia and, until his death in 1725, he attempted to create a strong, **westernized** state. He toured western Europe in 1697–8 and on his return to Russia he introduced many reforms to modernize his country, giving it new industries and an improved education system. After a lengthy war with Sweden which ended in 1721, Russia gained control of the Baltic Sea. A new capital city—St. Petersburg (Leningrad)—was built on the Baltic, which finally established Russia's presence in the West as a political power.

▲ The Palm Sunday parade in what is now Red Square in Moscow. The city clustered around the triangular fortress in the center, called the Kremlin. St. Basil's Cathedral (*on the left*) was built in the 1550s to celebrate the victories of Ivan the Fourth.

◀ Peter the Great in carpenter's dress. He traveled around Europe and learned shipbuilding techniques, which he later used to create a powerful Russian navy.

▼ Although the grand buildings of Russian cities were built of stone, the houses and churches of the Russian peasants were usually constructed with wooden logs.

▲ Peter the Great employed architects from all over Europe to design his new city of St. Petersburg. Built on a swampy site at the mouth of the River Neva, over 200,000 laborers died during its construction. The Winter Palace (*above*) was built by Peter's daughter, Elizabeth, who ruled Russia from 1741–62.

The state of Russia originally had its capital at Moscow, but Peter the Great extended his country to the Baltic Sea and created a new capital at St. Petersburg (Leningrad).

SWEDEN
Baltic Sea
POLAND
EUROPE
Black Sea
OTTOMAN EMPIRE

Archangel
St Petersburg (Leningrad)
Moscow
Muscovy
Caspian Sea
Bukhara

Ural Mountains

Siberia

RUSSIA

MONGOLIA

CHINA

— extent of Russian territory in 1533
--- extent of Russian territory in 1618
— extent of Russian territory in 1762

Kilometers
0   1000

0 miles   600

China

From 1368 to 1644 the Ming Dynasty ruled China. At first the Ming emperors brought order and stability to the vast country whose growing population was twice that of all Europe. But harvest failures and high taxes caused discontent and weakened the Empire, which was also being threatened by attacks from Japan, and by the Manchus, a highly organized tribe from Manchuria in the northeast.

In 1644 the Manchus invaded China and seized power, setting up a new imperial dynasty—the Ch'ing Dynasty. They strengthened the state and expanded it north into Mongolia and west into Tibet and Sinkiang. Trading links were established with Europe, and China exported porcelain, silk, cotton, and tea. However, the Chinese imported only gold and silver from Europe and continued to develop their own culture, so that by 1750, China was wealthy, secure, and quite independent of Europe.

Japan

During the 1400s and 1500s Japan was torn apart by civil war. But in 1603 peace was restored when one of the many warlords—Ieyasu Tokugawa—became **shogun**, or military leader, under the Emperor. Like China, Japan developed independently of the outside world. From 1639, all Christian missionaries were expelled, trade with Europe all but stopped and the Japanese were forbidden to go abroad.

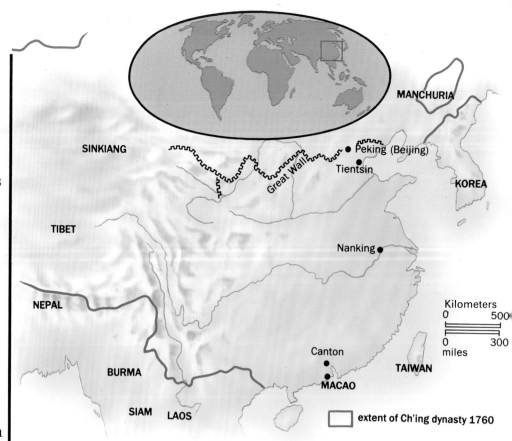

Both Ming blue-and-white ware (*right*), hand-made at the imperial factory, and the more basic pots and vases, manufactured in numerous small workshops all over China, were produced for the home market and for export to Europe. There they were highly prized for their fine design and were known as "china."

▲ Weaving silk on a loom. The Chinese silk industry was a vast enterprise, employing many thousands of workers, especially women, to produce silk textiles for home use and for export to Europe.

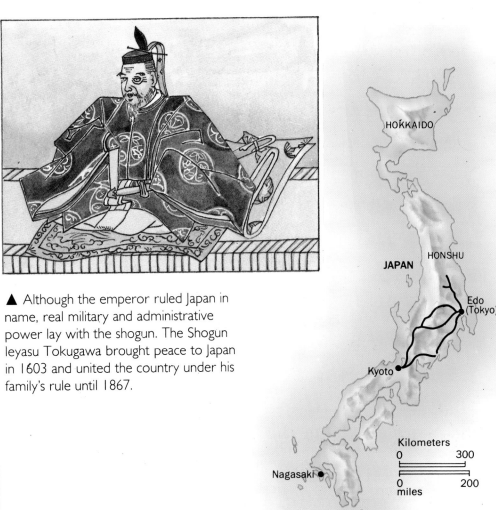

▲ Although the emperor ruled Japan in name, real military and administrative power lay with the shogun. The Shogun Ieyasu Tokugawa brought peace to Japan in 1603 and united the country under his family's rule until 1867.

HOKKAIDO

HONSHU

JAPAN

Edo (Tokyo)

Kyoto

Nagasaki

Kilometers
0   300

0   200
miles

— **Five highways**

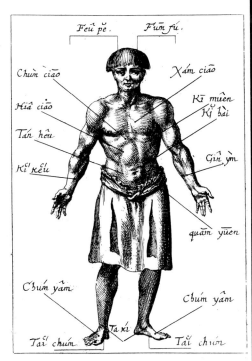

▲ Acupuncture—in which a number of fine needles are inserted into the skin to relieve pain and treat various ailments—has only recently been used in Western medicine, yet has been common practice in China for centuries.

▼ The elaborate ritual of dressing a *samurai*. The *samurai* were the aristocratic warrior class in Japan, famed for their bravery and devotion to the emperor. At one time they had the right to kill any commoner who offended them.

Australia and New Zealand

By 1700 Europeans had penetrated every part of the world. They had established trading links across the Atlantic and Pacific Oceans and had completely disrupted **indigenous** societies in the Americas, Southeast Asia and parts of Africa. Australia was the last "unknown continent" that the Europeans invaded.

Both the Aborigines in New Zealand had developed thriving societies based on a **nomadic** existence of hunting and fishing which had remained undisturbed by any contact with the outside world. This traditional way of life came to an end with the arrival of the Europeans. In 1605 the Dutch explorer, Willem Janszoon, became the first European to arrive in Australia, and in 1642 Abel Tasman sailed right around Australia.

Australia remained undisturbed until 1768, when the British Admiralty sent Captain James Cook to explore the continent. He made three voyages in all, claiming Australia for the British crown in 1770, and exploring the whole of the western Pacific. In 1788 the first Europeans settled in Australia, **convicts** transported from Britain to serve their sentences. These colonists soon overcame the powerless Aborigines. In 1840 a British settlement was established in New Zealand and the Maoris were forced to accept the rule of the British.

▲ One of the crew from Captain Cook's ship, the *Endeavour*, barters with a Maori in New Zealand for a crayfish.

▲ When he reached Australia, Captain Cook found many birds, animals and plants previously unknown in Europe. One of the animals was the kangaroo.

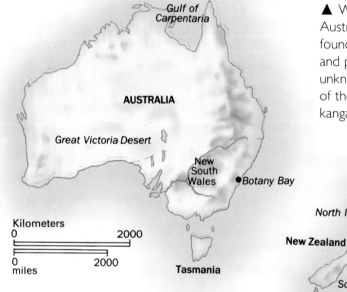

The Dutchman, Abel Tasman, set out in 1642 to find the fabled southern continent. He sailed right around Australia, proving that it was an island, and also discovered Tasmania, named after him, and New Zealand, which was named after the Dutch province of Zeeland.

▶ The Maoris came to New Zealand from the Pacific Islands in about A.D. 800, traditionally in seven canoes. By the 1700s they numbered about 100,000 people. This European drawing shows the son of a Maori chief, Otegoongoon, with his face "curiously tattooed."

Glossary

Absolute monarch A ruler such as Louis the Fourteenth who was completely responsible for governing a country.

Alliance A friendly agreement between peoples, groups, or countries.

Arable land Land which is plowed for growing crops.

Armada (means "fleet of warships") Usually describing the Spanish Armada which, in 1588, sailed against England.

Astrolabe An instrument for measuring the height of the stars above sea level. It was used by early navigators and sailors.

Authoritarian Expecting total obedience.

Balance of power A situation when two or more nations are equal in power.

Caribs The original peoples of the Caribbean.

Civilization An advanced stage in the development of a country.

Civil War A war between different groups of people within one country.

Colonize To found settlements abroad which are ruled or governed by the home country. Colonists are people who leave their home country to live in a colony.

Commerce Trade or buying and selling.

Common land A large piece of land, that can be used by anyone.

Conquistador (means "conqueror") The name given to the Spanish adventurers who sailed to South America in search of gold and riches.

Convict A person convicted or found guilty of being a criminal.

Culture Art, literature, music, and painting. Culture is also used to describe the way of life of the people of a country or region.

Dynasty A ruling family or series of rulers from one family.

Empire A group of countries under one ruler.

Excommunicate To expel someone from the Church.

French Revolution The Revolution in France against the royal family (1789–95).

Habsburgs The ruling house of Austria from the 1200s to the early 1900s.

Immunity The body's natural defense against disease.

Indigenous A word used to describe the native peoples of a country.

Irrigation A method of supplying dry land with water so that crops can grow.

Maroons Peoples of the Caribbean who are of mixed Caribbean and African origin.

Merchant economy This term is used to describe an economy based on trade.

Netherlands The name given to the kingdom of Holland.

New World A term used by the Europeans to describe the Americas.

Nomads People who move with their herds or flocks of animals in search of grazing land.

Pasture Land covered with grass used for grazing cattle or sheep.

Patron A wealthy supporter, usually of the arts.

Philosophy The study of the meaning of existence.

Plantation A large estate or area of land planted with trees or one crop such as sugar beet, tea, tobacco, or cotton.

Renaissance (means "rebirth") A period of European history from the 1400s to the 1600s when people rediscovered the learning and work of the Ancient Greeks and Romans.

Republic A country with an elected government but no royal family.

Shogun Military ruler of Japan.

Spice Islands The islands of Southeast Asia from where spices were exported to Europe.

State A country or a part of a country which governs its own affairs.

Treaty A written agreement between one or more countries.

Triangular trade The sea trade in slaves and goods in the 1600s and 1700s.

Tsar A Russian word meaning "emperor" used to describe the rulers of Russia.

Westernized A word used to describe countries or ways of life that have been influenced by the Western part of the world such as the United States or Europe.

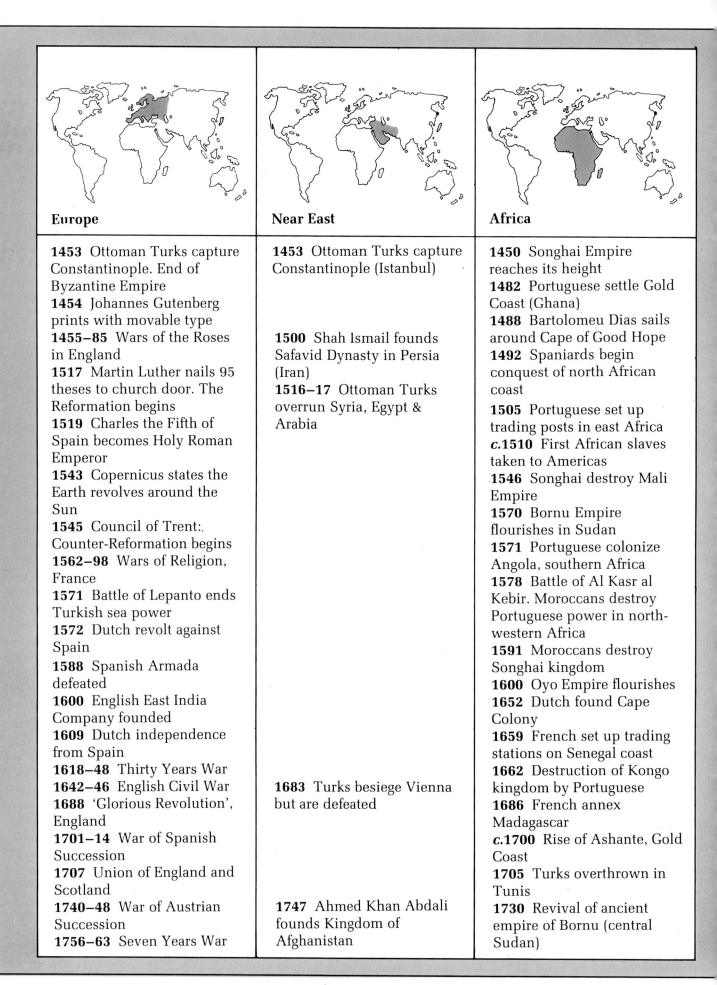

Europe

1453 Ottoman Turks capture Constantinople. End of Byzantine Empire
1454 Johannes Gutenberg prints with movable type
1455–85 Wars of the Roses in England
1517 Martin Luther nails 95 theses to church door. The Reformation begins
1519 Charles the Fifth of Spain becomes Holy Roman Emperor
1543 Copernicus states the Earth revolves around the Sun
1545 Council of Trent: Counter-Reformation begins
1562–98 Wars of Religion, France
1571 Battle of Lepanto ends Turkish sea power
1572 Dutch revolt against Spain
1588 Spanish Armada defeated
1600 English East India Company founded
1609 Dutch independence from Spain
1618–48 Thirty Years War
1642–46 English Civil War
1688 'Glorious Revolution', England
1701–14 War of Spanish Succession
1707 Union of England and Scotland
1740–48 War of Austrian Succession
1756–63 Seven Years War

Near East

1453 Ottoman Turks capture Constantinople (Istanbul)

1500 Shah Ismail founds Safavid Dynasty in Persia (Iran)
1516–17 Ottoman Turks overrun Syria, Egypt & Arabia

1683 Turks besiege Vienna but are defeated

1747 Ahmed Khan Abdali founds Kingdom of Afghanistan

Africa

1450 Songhai Empire reaches its height
1482 Portuguese settle Gold Coast (Ghana)
1488 Bartolomeu Dias sails around Cape of Good Hope
1492 Spaniards begin conquest of north African coast
1505 Portuguese set up trading posts in east Africa
*c.***1510** First African slaves taken to Americas
1546 Songhai destroy Mali Empire
1570 Bornu Empire flourishes in Sudan
1571 Portuguese colonize Angola, southern Africa
1578 Battle of Al Kasr al Kebir. Moroccans destroy Portuguese power in north-western Africa
1591 Moroccans destroy Songhai kingdom
1600 Oyo Empire flourishes
1652 Dutch found Cape Colony
1659 French set up trading stations on Senegal coast
1662 Destruction of Kongo kingdom by Portuguese
1686 French annex Madagascar
*c.***1700** Rise of Ashante, Gold Coast
1705 Turks overthrown in Tunis
1730 Revival of ancient empire of Bornu (central Sudan)

Asia & the Far East	The Americas	Australasia

Asia & the Far East

1471 Vietnamese expand southward

1498 Vasco da Gama reaches India via Cape of Good Hope

1519 Nanak founds Sikh religion in India

1526 Babur conquers Delhi and founds Mughal Empire

1550 Mongol Altan Khan invades northern China

1592–3, 1597–8 Japan invades Korea but is expelled by China

*c.***1608** Tokugawa period begins in Japan

1608 Confucianism becomes official religion in Japan

1619 Portuguese found Batavia (Jakarta)

1630s Japan isolates itself from the rest of the world

1644 Manchus found Ch'in Dynasty, China

1648 Taj Mahal completed, India

1649 Russians reach Pacific and found Okhotsk

1690 Calcutta founded by British in India

*c.***1690** Russia expands to Black Sea

1697 Chinese occupy Outer Mongolia

1707 Death of Aurangzeb, decline of Mughal Empire, India

1708 Sikhs rule Punjab

1720 Manchus rule in Tibet

1736 Nader Shah deposes Safavid Dynasty

1751 China overruns Tibet

The Americas

1438 Inca Empire established, Peru

1440–69 Montezuma rules Aztec Empire

1492 Columbus reaches Carribean

1494 Treaty of Tordesillas divides Americas between Portugal and Spain

1497 Cabot reaches Newfoundland

1520 Magellan crosses Pacific Ocean

1521 Cortés conquers Aztec capital Tenochtitlán

1533 Pizarro conquers Peru

1545 Discovery of silver mines in Peru and Mexico

*c.***1560** Portuguese set up sugar plantations in Brazil

1607 First English settlement in America (Jamestown, Virginia)

1608 French colonists found Quebec

1620 Puritans on *Mayflower* land in New England

1624 Dutch settle New Amsterdam

1636 Harvard College founded – first university in America

1664 British seize New Amsterdam, re-name it New York

1684 La Salle explores Mississippi. Claims Louisiana for France

1728 Bering explores Alaska

1759 British capture Quebec from French.

Australasia

1642 Tasman reaches New Zealand and Tasmania

1768 James Cook explores Pacific

Index

Moscow 36, *36*, 37
Mughal Empire 8, 24, *24*, 25, *25*
Muslims *see* Islam

navigation at sea 13, *13*
Netherlands 16, 17, 20, *20*, 24;
    "New World" 26, 28, *28*;
    Tasman 40
New Amsterdam 28, *28*
New England 26, 28
"New World" *see* Americas, the
New Zealand 40
Newton, Isaac 33, *33*
nomads 40
nuns 21

Osman the First, Ottoman king 22
Ottoman Empire 18, 22, *22*, 23, *23*

Persia, Savafid Empire of 22
Peter the Great, Tsar of Russia 36, *36*
Philip the Second, King of Spain 16
Pilgrim Fathers 27, *27*
Pizarro, Francisco 14
plantations 16, 26, 29
plows 20, *20*
porcelain 38, *38*
Portugal: colonization 16, *16*, 17,
    24; exploration 12, 14; "New
    World" 26; slave trade 29, 30, 31
potatoes 20
printing 10, 11, *11*
Protestantism 18–19, 32
Ptolemy, Claudius 12, *12*
Puritans 27, *27*, 32

Quetzalcoatl 8, *8*

Raphael 10
Reformation 18, 33
religions: Hindus 24; Islam
    (Muslims) 10, 22, 23, *23*, 24, 30;
    Protestants 18–19, 32; Puritans
    27, *27*, 32; Roman Catholics
    18–19, 32, 33, 35; Sikhs 24, *24*
Renaissance Europe 10, 33
Roman Catholics 18–19, 32, 33, 35
Russia 18, 36–7

Safavid Empire 22
St. Lucia 16, *16*

St. Peter's Church (Rome) 19, *19*
St. Petersburg 36, 37, *37*
St. Sophia (Istanbul) 23, *23*
salons 34, *34*
samurai (warrior) 39, *39*
Santa Maria (ship), 12, *12*
science 10, 33, 35
Shi'ite Muslims 22
ships 12, *12*, 13, *13*, 27, *27*, 29, *29*
Siberia 36
Sikhs 24, *24*
silks 12, 38, 39, *39*
silver 14, *14*, 16, 26, 38
slavery 16, 26–7, 29, *29*
Solar System 33, *33*
Spain: colonization 16, *16*;
    conquistadors 14, *14*, 20;
    exploration 12; "New World 26;
    War of the Spanish Succession
    32
Spice Islands 16, 17, *17*
spices 12, 13, 17, *17*
sugar 17, 29
Suleiman (Ottoman Emperor) 23, *23*
Sunni Muslims 22
Sweden 36

Taj Mahal 25, *25*
Tasman, Abel 40

tea 17, 25, *25*, 38
Tenochtitlán 14, 15, *15*
Thirty Years War 32
Timbuctu 31, *31*
tobacco 17, 26, *26*, 29
Tokugawa, Ieyasu 38, 39, *39*
trade 8, 12, 16, 20, 24, 25, 28, 30,
    38, 40; slave trade 29, *29*, 30
trappers 27, 28, *28*
Turkey *see* Ottoman Empire

United States of America 26
Ursulines 21

Vasco da Gama 12, 13, *13*
Versailles, Palace of 34, 35, *35*
Vesalius 33
Vespucci, Amerigo 13, *13*
Virginia 26

War of the Spanish Succession 32
West Indies 12, 13, 14, 16, *16*, 29,
    34
White, John 27
Winter Palace (St Petersburg) 37, *37*
witches 21
women 21, *21*, 22, *22*, 25, *25*, 34

Acknowledgments

The publishers wish to thank the following for supplying photographs for this book:
Page 9 The Hutchison Library; 10 Michael Holford; 11 The Mansell Collection; 12 Michael Holford; 14 South American Pictures; 15 Peter Newark's Pictures (top), British Museum (bottom); 16 Werner Forman Archive (top), National Maritime Museum (bottom); 17 The Mansell Collection; 18 Ancient Art & Architecture Collection; 19 ZEFA (top), The National Gallery (middle), The Mansell Collection (bottom); 20 Vienna Art History Museum; 21 Mary Evans Picture Library; 23 Bodleian Library, Oxford (top left), Sonia Halliday Photographs (top right), ZEFA (bottom); 24 ZEFA; 25 Werner Forman Archive (top), Michael Holford (bottom left), ZEFA (bottom right); 27 Peter Newark's Pictures (top left and bottom), British Museum (top right); 28 The Mansell Collection (top), British Library (bottom); Peter Newark's Pictures (right), Mary Evans Picture Library (bottom); 30 Peter Newark's Pictures (top left), Werner Forman Archive (bottom); 31 Hulton Picture Company; 33 Ann Ronan Picture Library (top), The Mansell Collection (bottom); 34 The Wallace Collection (top), Giraudon (bottom); 35 Picturepoint (top), Mary Evans Picture Library (bottom); 36 Fotomas Index (top and bottom), Michael Holford (middle); 37 ZEFA; 38 Fotomas Index; 39 Michael Holford (top), Mary Evans Picture Library (bottom left), Hulton Picture Company (bottom right); 40 British Library (top), Fotomas Index (bottom).
Front Cover South American Pictures
Back Cover Vienna Art History Museum
Endpapers Michael Holford